BE YOU,

By
Tonya Lewis Taylor

DEDICATION

I dedicate this book to my family: My amazing husband, JP Taylor,
I thank you for your love and unwavering support. My children, Jamiah,
Jaila, Jahna, and Jaden, you make me better, you are my joy. My awesome
parents, Deacon Victor Lewis and Dr. Dorothy Lewis for helping
me become the woman I am today. My sister, Kecia, and all my sister girls
who hold me down, I could not make this journey without you!
To all my friends and extended family who have always supported me,
I love you all forever!

I want to recognize five of the strongest women who helped shape my destiny:
Mamie Moore Mitchell (maternal grandmother, deceased), Anna Lewis
(paternal grandmother, deceased), Emma Burnet (grandaunt, deceased),
Annie Mae Sealy (aunt, deceased), and Mother Francis Galloway (my first
Pastor, deceased).

Lastly, this book is dedicated to all the women who struggle to just be
themselves. Be unapologetically You, Not Her.

CONTENTS

Introduction

INTRODUCTION

Have you ever wondered what qualities the most successful people in the world possess? More than money, talent, fame, or power, you will find that they have discovered the secret to what makes them who they are. There is underneath usually a foundation of self-confidence, inner faith, and a unique spirit that makes them stand above average. This is not because they are better than you or me, but because they have asked and understood these questions:

Who am I?

Why am I here?

How do my unique gifts and talents fit into the world?

The world currently holds over seven billion human beings. Yet how many of us are actually human beings with no clue on how to BE. I've seen so many people, especially women, who have no clue about who they are. They are busy being mothers, wives, students, doctors, lawyers, sisters, daughters, and friends. How do I know this? Well, it's because I was one of those women unaware of what I was created to do.

I grew up during a time when you were told what to do and you just did it. I grew up in a Christian home with both my parents in ministry. So, we learned how to serve and just do whatever was needed to help build God's kingdom here on earth. If they needed you to sing, you sang, if they needed you to preach, you preached. If they needed you to fry chicken—you fried that chicken! You were taught to serve.

Now, I'm not saying that the years I spent serving in ministry contributed to me not understanding who I was, but I do believe being so busy didn't allow me to answer two essential questions—ones that would dictate the trajectory of my life and determine my destiny:

Who am I and why am I here?

The answers to those questions will revolutionize how you view your life and how your unique gifts and talents fit into the world. Everything you are and every experience you have been through in your life are based on these questions. Your decisions and the people you are connected to are all based on them as well.

Why? Because we attract the destiny, we want by who we believe we are. If you haven't taken the time to determine who we are, you will attract inconsistency in your life and never really become who you were destined to be.

BE YOU, NOT HER grew out of many years of self-assessment. I grew up always feeling like there was something wrong with me. My personality, my hair, face and eyes, down to my thighs, and even my cleaning obsession (Yes, I said cleaning obsession—that's another book). I would always compare myself to other women as a metric for my life's journey. I always doubted myself, and I would say, "I wish I was her size, or I wish I had hair like her or I wish I could sing like her..."

What I didn't realize by constantly comparing my life to someone else's life, I realized that I had not taken the time to define myself. So, I went on a journey that I'm almost embarrassed to admit lasted ten years. But I was determined to like and love myself. This meant dedication to examining myself and finding out who Tonya Lewis Taylor really is and why she is here.

Once I started to understand these questions, it was then and only then that I began to BE ME!

Once you understand who you are and why you're here, there is no need to compare yourself to anyone else because everything you are is exactly what you're supposed to be. I decided to write this book to celebrate my journey of self-discovery and to inspire and encourage women like me who struggle with insecurities. As you read this book, I hope you will celebrate your uniqueness and also to be inspired to BE YOU, NOT HER. I'm a church girl, and there's an old hymn that starts off with this phrase, "*Life is filled with swift transitions…*"—this is so true. Our world is constantly changing and evolving. It is almost impossible to keep up. I grew up in a simpler time. There was no internet or social media (and no, I'm not that old). People called you on the phone and had a conversation with you instead of sending a text. But now we must keep up with the fast-paced, ever-changing world we live in.

There is so much pressure around us to conform to a standard to "*be like her.*" Being like her takes a lack of originality because you're directed to stick to *her* script, follow *her* blueprint—for life. Even the beauty industry has made it impossible to be unique. The industry has a standard of beauty to sell, and everyone is buying into it. Social media takes this to another level.

Everyone looks and acts alike in this arena. There are tutorials on how to do just that—get your eyebrows on "fleek," how to look like the hottest Instagram model, and how to be in style. That's not only a fad or a trend, it's a box. For every YouTube video or "social media influencer" telling you how to remake your entire face into one that everyone will love, there

is a mirror somewhere begging you to stay *you*.

Lately, we see more body dysmorphia, not just correcting what may

be a minor flaw, but overly enhancing and exaggerating physical features;

and it's a dangerous new trend.

More than ever, we see these examples of extreme surgeries/injections

happening around us, and even the botched results that sometimes follow,

being displayed all over the internet. Some of us wonder, "Why would

anyone do that to themselves? They looked just fine before!" We scratch

our heads when the facial features of celebrities change, when their whole

look becomes something other than how they started out, and those who

are not emotionally secure follow their example. Social media is not evil

and it's not wrong to use, but showing us these trends in HD is certainly a

trapdoor for insecure people to fall through.

At the beginning of this book, I said that the most successful people in

the world has learned to just be themselves and still find success.

Whoopi Goldberg is a classic example of a person who has remained her

authentic self. She moves to her own beat and makes her own rules.

She dresses and wears her hair the way she likes, and with her shaved eyebrows, she has made Hollywood adapt and adjust to her uniqueness.

Never once did you see Whoopi conform to *Being Her*—as in that other woman—but instead she clearly projects the essence of who she is. These people step outside the norm: They know who they are and why they were created. You see it when you look at them being celebrated for their talents, brilliance, or service. You are looking at a shine that comes from inside and works its way up, and what you see is them *working* it! Speaking of working, with so much to DO, here is a reminder that there are many distractions that will sidetrack you, making you so busy outside and never addressing these questions inside. There are times when you may want to give up, but anything worth having you must push hard to accomplish. Often, we need a guide and uplifting reminder not just to stay driven toward our purpose, but to stay empowered.

That is what I put into every page of this book—the power to be you.

The goal of *being you not her* covers everything from:

How you wear your hair…

How you dress…

How you speak…

To your sense of humor...

I've always been a multi-dimensional person. For example, I'm an introvert, but I'm a people-person when I'm around people. I'm very direct and to the point, and yet I am a compassionate listener. These qualities have always seemed extreme to me, but my lifestyle dictates that I be myself. Everything I am is what I have to express openly—otherwise, I feel stifled. I've *got* to be me.

In researching for this book, I realized that women are being driven to insanity with the rollercoaster fads and fiction behind what a woman is supposed to be.

Here is where you focus on your inner self before you undertake any other mission. Focusing not on your roles, your career, society, or the demands that may come with all that, but instead on who shows up for that role. The mission must start somewhere, ladies, why not start inside?

BE YOU NOT HER,

TLT

I ENJOY THE BLESSINGS I GET FROM BEING MYSELF.

Be You, Not Her

CHAPTER ONE
BE YOU

✓ Who Are You, Really?
✓ Created in His Image
✓ There's Nobody Like You
✓ Unleash the Inner You
✓ Forget the Past
✓ Accept Who You Are

WHO ARE YOU, REALLY?

Wait, before you answer with what defining roles you fill—*woman, mother, daughter, wife, sister, friend, singer, pastor, business owner,* etc.—I want you to dig a little bit deeper. That's because it's one of the most important questions you could ever ask yourself: "Who am I?" Have you spent time with yourself long enough to truly define, not just the role, but the depths of who is acting it out? Who you are underneath the role you play determines how you carry it out. The truth of you will surface in everything you do.

BE YOU

As a woman living in this day and age, we have too many things to deal with—again, human doings instead of human beings. We wear too many hats, and sometimes the lines are blurred, and we lose sight of who we are. This isn't new. Years ago, women's roles were well-defined. We were homemakers who cared for the household, and we were the primary caretakers of the children, while the fathers went to work every day. The word *matrimony* itself basically defines exactly what a woman's role should be. At its Latin root, the word *matrimonium* came from "mater," or "mother," while the suffix *–monium* described an action or condition by which a woman was to act and be in the state of both mother and wife. So, if you married someone, you signed up for this action-for life. Accepting this role, the mother had a simple existence: she cooked, cleaned, and made sure the children were okay. She cared for the entire family sunup to sundown. In every culture, the role of mother and even "woman" was established as one set in stone. Although not as rigid, even today, a homemaker's job is no easy task. For many women who are stay-at-home moms, work is never done. But compared to today, the work of an average woman at home caring for her family was certainly, harder before the 1960s.

That era ushered in a new age of independence for women.

Women became strong, independent, and determined to do what men did. We wanted to have the career, but we also wanted a family. That led to climbing the corporate ladder to try and make over six figures and be accepted as equals in business. We should be allowed to do these things because we can, and yet everything comes with a price. To enjoy the successes of being a working woman and the joys of being a wife and raising children, there will be a sacrifice. The demands of taking on so many responsibilities come at our own expense. You look up and you're a human doing way too much.

So, I ask this question once again, "Who are you?," so that you can in turn ask yourself. What sort of *being* is doing what you're doing? Once you ask this question inwardly, and honestly, without including the roles you play…well, you know… the truth will set you free—so there you have it! The lesson of this story is how to, at the end of the day, be free. From what? Overdoing everything like a slave to a role society has set up for you. From every direction that points you away from you and toward a standard that doesn't even fit—like *her* clothes if you tried to put them on.

Unless we define who, we are, we can never truly be the women we were destined to be as individuals. There might be a collective destiny for all women as we reposition for equal power and respect, but it begins with a singular journey. It starts with each one of us bringing our unique strengths to the cause. We must first strip ourselves down and discover the person inside, not the person the world sees, all in order to define that uniqueness. Your goal is to be the best you can be, but how can that happen if you don't even know who you are to begin with? We are like a fish out of water, just flapping around, going nowhere, without self-knowledge. But there is somewhere to go—inward. The original, authentic YOU is in there. You will see she doesn't look, sound, or act like a cookie cutter version of other women, and that's just fine. In fact, that's our goal.

THOUGHT EXERCISE

Today I must examine myself and ask myself, *who am I?*

What do I like?

What don't I like?

Do I like what I have become?

Do I like what I see in the mirror?

Am I living my best life, or is there room for improvement?

CREATED IN HIS IMAGE

We were made in the reflection of a perfect image. While inside your inner thoughts, remember that fact first, because the ideas that you need to carry you forward are based on such perfection. It's your north star on the journey. You can't get lost if you remember: *I was conceived and planted here by purpose, on purpose, and for a purpose by a most perfect Creator. How can I be made wrong?*

THERE'S NOBODY LIKE YOU

Not only have scientists found that we all have a unique fingerprint, they've also found that no two humans have the same tongue print in addition to other unique qualities that make you, YOU, and her, HER. That means it should be easy to just be yourself, since you can't copy another individual to the letter anyway.

Only it ain't easy. In fact, it's made even harder because it's bigger business to sell that cookie cutter life—look like, live like, think like, spend like, be like... *her*. And can I tell you something? That standard of her that they're selling—she ain't even real! For a woman who is trying to keep her authenticity, she must maneuver past all that pressure and define something that is her own: Question, what is unique to you that you are proud of or should be?

UNLEASH THE INNER YOU

You are pent up, repressed, held back, and marginalized—at least according to society. But that's addressing the many roles women play, not the freedom you actually possess inwardly. Women have been traditionally limited in career possibilities, and the demands of motherhood (especially single motherhood) which place even greater and more restrictions on their potential. But your inner possibility is not on a leash. It has no limits on setting goals or empowering your spirit to

go after them.

When you unlock the door to your own inner possibilities and unleash yourself, you'll find you are in the company of women who have defied the odds and became legends. Maya Angelou, Oprah Winfrey, Serena Williams, Iyanla Vanzant, Whoopi Goldberg, and many others who endured great difficulties to become household names you may have just recognized right off the page.

You are writing your own future legacy onto the pages of life, and you've got to bring forth your truest and best representation. The one hidden UNDER the roles you play.

One day I was watching television, and I heard a preacher say, "If you allowed me to develop into the person that I really am there is nothing I could not accomplish in this life." When I heard that statement, I realized that most of us are living someone else's life. Most of us spend much of our time developing the outer shell so much that the inner person gets lost.

We girls are big on looking our best. We make sure our outward appearance is just fine. We go to the salon weekly, and we make sure our manicured nails are kept looking picture perfect—lace fronts give the perfect polished hair do and our clothes have to fit just right.... Ultimate Perfection. But.... I've learned if you just let, go and allow the person inside to shine through, you'd be surprised at what you could accomplish. I am an advocate of looking my best but what I am saying that the superficial things can be a distraction if you're not taking time to focus on the inner things.

Most of us have struggled at some point during our lives with being the person that no one sees. We are taught as little girls to fit into a mold that is reserved for others. Sometimes, we spend years of our lives living a marked-down version of who we really are. We settle for much less than our true worth because we are afraid to walk into our authentic destiny.

It is my belief that everyone is conflicted at times with our inner person. Yet that inward person contains the essence of the woman you really are, SHE simply needs awareness of who or what is causing such conflicts. What we see as the outer appearance is just the representative, we offer the world. It's a fixed image and personality that both adjust to get along best in the world. It's usually something people will like and accept and hopefully even love, even if it isn't authentic—just so long as it works. This acceptable modified version of you exists because we are taught that if we display all of who we really are, no one would like us for that raw truth. But isn't it time to break free of the chains that bind us and instead, by self-discovery, redefine us?

When you surface out of your self-awareness, you will realize that you are fearfully and wonderfully made and that there is no one like you. That realization is direct permission to Be You. Then you can find a way to break out of the box that is holding back your progress.

I realized that we had a problem in our society a few years ago when several plastic surgery television shows popped up on television.

The larger rear ends, fuller lips, bigger boobs, nose jobs, cheek implants, and other morphing's were happening across the racial spectrum and were both creating and fueling a fascination with female acceptance and cultural appropriation. Should a nose native to your ethnicity be modified to look like that of another race. Should someone of one identified race be able to adopt the looks that were once dismissed as being unattractive in another? I am not saying that every person who has undergone plastic surgery had self-esteem issues or is trying to be someone else. But when I hear a person say, "Give me Angelina Jolie's lips or Jennifer Lopez's rear end," then it has become clear that there is an issue with accepting what is native to you and your natural form. Is this a problem in our society? You tell me…

FORGET THE PAST

If you ask me, we have a whole lotta time travelers hanging around, because what is supposed to be scientifically impossible is happening every minute. Some poor mind is skyrocketing backward to *woulda, coulda,*

shoulda feelings due to a memory from their deep past. Usually, these memories are negative or painful, even when you are just combing through the good ones and *whoops!* hit a bad one. Because the rainy days are tucked beneath your past too, and it is almost impossible to avoid them. These memories are just like that picture you hate in the family photo album, that one you cringe at. There are parts of your past that you wish you could rip out or rush past and ignore, just like those pictures. How do you forget the negative and still cherish the good parts of your past?

One thing is to keep as much mental focus on staying grounded where you are in the present. Even the best memories are still anchored to what WAS and don't allow us to ride the current of what IS. When you stay in the current, not even thinking too much about tomorrow other than setting a goal for it and aiming, you won't have much time for the past. Those memories are persistent because you keep knocking on the door to yesterday, and those old recollections are dressed and ready to greet you for a long visit. It's ready to open you up to distractions and delays—even with the fun recalls. But do you have time for all that?

Believe me, I know letting go of the past is probably the biggest step a person will ever take in their life. Most of us are dealing with something in our past that we are still trying to get over 20 years later. Heavy, deep stuff. Most of us come from one type of dysfunctional circumstance or another. It doesn't matter if you were born into the poorest conditions or the wealthiest family, we all have something in our past that, if not challenged, can bring forth negativity in the future.

A woman shared with me that she was abused as a child, and it caused her to have emotional baggage when it comes to relationships, even today. She said, "I am very distrusting, and I always seem to choose men who are controlling."

A friend of mine told me that when she was a little girl, her mom used to give her very small portions of food, rationing out everything she ate because money was tight. She told me that there were many nights when she went to bed hungry because she wanted more food, but her mother told her "no." As an adult, she became overweight because she had decided to never deprive herself of food again, and she has since struggled in a 20-year battle over her weight and overindulgence in food.

Another story comes to mind of a woman who was constantly compared to her younger sister and, as a result, grew up feeling that she was not pretty enough because she did not fit *their* description of beauty. As a result, she always had a complex about her looks, never discovering her own true beauty, instead always looking at others to measure it. I am

sure, if we all think hard, we can find countless instances in our own lives when things from our past re-presented themselves. Again, I am not suggesting that everything from yesteryear should be overlooked, I am merely pointing out that only the negativity seems to emerge when you do go there, so be careful.

For example, Anita was raped when she was 14 years old. She and some friends cut school and went to the party of a classmate while their parents were working. Anita went to the bathroom while the others continued to indulge in drinking and risqué behaviors with those in the other room. Once in the bathroom, the older brother of the host forced his way in and pulled out a gun. He informed Anita that if she didn't do exactly what he said, he would kill her. Out of terror, Anita performed some of the most disgusting sexual acts at the hands of her abuser. When the assault was finished, he made her clean herself up and go back to the party, telling her that if she mentioned anything to anyone he would find her and kill her. Anita went back to the party, and no one had even noticed she was gone. Despite what seemed like hours of sexual abuse, she had only been gone for ten minutes. She informed the person who brought her to the party that she needed to go home, but she did not let on that anything was wrong. When Anita got home, she immediately broke down and wept. She became so distraught that she faked being sick and stayed home from school. Fast forward… Anita is twenty-five, and the damage from the rape has made her develop a distrust of men. All through college, she continued to allow the tragedies of her past to control her present choices. She could never forgive or forget the abuser, and because of the problems she faced, Anita hasn't been able to develop trusting relationships. Any young gentleman who has been interested in dating her has been pushed aside because of her mistrust of all men.

It is not easy to let go of the past, especially when we have been hurt, but it is necessary in order to move into your destiny. Letting go includes all the hurt and pain that have shaped our lives. Many women have faced insurmountable challenges, but we can never allow our yesterday to dictate our today and tomorrow. Sometimes, we can get caught up in a pity party and even begin to question God.

I am reminded of the woman by the name of Charlie who was attacked by a chimpanzee. The animal literally ripped her face off. On the Oprah Winfrey Show, she revealed her injuries to the entire world. I remember crying as she lifted the veil from her face to expose the damage that had been done by the animal. I stood in front of the television, numb, until she started to speak: "I don't have time to sit here and hold a grudge or pity myself. I have to stay positive so I can heal myself."

I realized at that moment all that we take much for granted—a little pimple here or a wrinkle there, which is nothing in comparison to what this woman deals with daily. Yet Charlie realized that if she didn't let go of her past, she could not heal or embrace her future possibilities.

ACCEPT WHO YOU ARE

As of right now, today, deal with the man in the mirror, so to speak. Right now, get up, go look in the nearest mirror and say, honestly, if you accept who is staring back—flaws and all, ya'll! Is she acceptable, worthy, capable, possible, self-loved? If she isn't, it's time to dig deeper.

Self-acceptance is probably one of the hardest tasks I have ever had to accomplish in my life. It required me to take a real serious look at myself. Not just the outer me, but the inner me. You must really understand who you are and what you have been given during this self-examination process. You have to literally take apart the person in the mirror and uncover the deepest, darkest secrets of your personality. Anything that you don't like, you must literally face.

I promise you it is the most difficult and challenging task I have ever completed in my entire life. It is worse than giving birth—and mothers, you know that hurts! It is worse than anything you could imagine, because most people don't want to deal with all the issues and problems that make them who they are. Every tear you shed, each difficult situation, all your family issues—these must be faced head on and accepted as fixable, disposable, or forgettable.

As a youth, I was overweight and always struggled with it. As a young teen, during those impressionable years, I often felt like the fat friend. You know, the one that everyone overlooks because all the other friends are a size 2 or some other ridiculously low number. When I look back at my pictures, I wasn't fat at all. I had a very adult frame for a teenager, but I wasn't fat. That was just one of many insecurities—mostly based on comparisons with HER and not ME.

I would confide in my older sister Kecia and ask questions like, Am I ugly? Am I fat? Why is my hair short? And every time she would look at me and say, "Tonya, you are who you are." And every time she'd say that to me, I would get furious; I mean fighting mad. She'd ask, "Why are you angry at me? I'm just telling you the truth," and I'd say, "Because you won't answer my question." She'd reply, "Because it doesn't matter what I tell you, it matters what you believe. It doesn't matter what I see, it matters what *you* see."

It would be 20 years before I began to understand what she was talking about. Just a few years ago, I entered an era of self-acceptance in my life. Yet throughout the course of my growth, I had to deal with many such insecurities, until I realized, one day, that I didn't care who liked me or who didn't... I liked myself. I did my personal inventory:

"I like my slim hips and big breasts, my almond-shaped eyes and full cheeks. I like my laugh, my smile, and my personality. I'm kind, compassionate, and giving, but I'm not a pushover. I like the fact that I am direct. a self-starter, and resilient, even like that I'm a little too chatty at times"... in other words, I like Tonya!

What is your personal inventory?

You should take one for yourself as well, because many women have not gotten to the point where they don't like who they are. Because to do that, they would have to deal with all the pain and scars of the past, and many of them don't want to face what is too ugly to view. It's not easy dealing with all your crazy stuff, but it is so necessary to do in order to have a clear and present life. This particular mental quality of self-acceptance is one that you will really have to stay on top of with every vision, goal, and desire for your life. Your life will never be the same once you accept who you are and utilize those qualities to literally walk toward your destiny. No one can stop you except you when you stop! No one can block you once you understand who you are—as defined by you.

I STRIVE TO BE
MY BETTER SELF.
I WILL DO EVERYTHING
TO THE BEST OF
MY ABILITY.

Be You, Not Her

CHAPTER TWO
BE EXCELLENT

✓ Define Your Personal Excellence
✓ Principles of Excellence
✓ Invest in Quality
✓ Let Your Light Shine
✓ Be Committed to the Process

DEFINE YOUR PERSONAL EXCELLENCE

As a woman of excellence who strives to be the best, she can be in every area and role, she understands that everything that is God-given in her requires her to do her best in expressing it. She has the inner beauty, creativity, and sense of style to create success in her life and the lives of her loved ones. Now the goal is to push that to all that it can be—because you CAN. My wish for all women is for excellence to be a part of our daily thinking. When we do something, we should ask, "Does it represent excellence?"

exceeding, exceedingly; pre-eminent, surpassing, extreme, extraordinary
Ex•cel•lence noun
The state, quality, or condition of excelling; superiority; Something in which one excels. ex•cel, ex•celled, ex•cel•ling, ex•cels verb, transitive: To do or be better than or surpass; To show superiority. Synonyms: excel, surpass, exceed, transcend, outdo.

These definitions mean to be or go beyond a limit or standard, and that includes the ones society has set for women. Excellence is not a natural gift but rather it's an enhancement. It must be pursued and sought after as you would a goal to be reached.

You will know it when it arrives by the fruits that you eventually bear.

PRINCIPLES OF EXCELLENCE:

"Make the original worth copying. Do it right the first time."

"Many times, the difference between failure and success is doing something nearly right... or doing it exactly right."

INVEST IN QUALITY

"Excellence always endures... it remains long after cost is forgotten."

"The satisfaction of quality far outweighs the bitterness of a cheap imitation."

LET YOUR LIGHT SHINE

There is a song we have all heard, "This little light of mine... I'm gonna let it shine…" When you think about the song, in order for this light to shine, it has to be burning brightly and have enough oil and/or batteries to continue to blaze. As women, we must let our light illuminate even the rooms we enter, the positions we fill, and the tasks we undertake, so that wherever we go, people will notice us and not her.

Why would I say this? Because, as women, we have a tendency to let our light go dim, often due to intimidation from the lights shining from other women. The light in each one of us has its own purpose focus and destiny. Yet sometimes with the demands of life, we forget that we must replenish our glow on a daily basis. Batteries have to be recharged and oil replenished. We are always on the go as mothers, wives, sisters, aunts, friends, business owners, etc., and sometimes, if we are not careful, we can get burned out in our roles. In other words, you can lose your zeal.

I am reminded of a woman who is a pastor of a congregation. When she and her husband first started their ministry, she had such great hopes and expectations. She was on fire for the Lord! Her ministry was growing, and she was helping so many people in her community. She would run revivals where people would be saved, she even became an in-demand speaker. This meant extensive travel all over the country, ministering to people about their pain and hurt. At one point, she was even asked to do a television program and a radio show.

Her light was shining brightly. A few years later, she fell off the scene, she was all burned out. The demands of her ministry became too much. Her light began to grow dim and she has fallen away from ministry. As women, we must understand that our strength is in our ability to shine through the darkness. Women, we have a natural glow and we cannot let the harshness of the world or its demands cause us to lose our light. Come on sisters, shine let it shine!

BE COMMITTED TO THE PROCESS

Becoming the woman, you always wanted to be requires a serious commitment to yourself. This is not some quick "overnight you are healed" process. Becoming the woman, you want to be is a step-by-step maneuver you have to be patient with. Just like it takes time to make a cake, your steps include having the right ingredients beforehand, and then stirring and mixing them, even before you bake them. If you take it out of the oven before it is fully cooked; you can ruin the entire cake. So, it is with your process of becoming the person you are committed to be. You should gather your uniqueness, push it toward excellence, and then allow the proper time needed to be a finished product—and even then, you must allow time for it to cool before serving the world your best version of you. When you make a commitment to yourself, you are saying

that you are willing to be faithful and true. You will be devoted to seeing goals through to the end of the process. It is much like a man and woman preparing for marriage. Repeat this to yourself:

"I, (name), am committed to becoming the woman God has created me to be. I am aware that my experiences in life, whether good, bad, or indifferent, have shaped and molded me into becoming who I am destined to be. I also know the road is not going to be easy, as there will be good times and bad times, there will be sickness and health, there will be joy and sorrow… But I promise to offer myself to God's highest vision for me."

The two most important relationships are between God and with us. Your relationship with yourself is important, because you must get to know and understand your God-given gifts and talents. You must understand what problems you were created to solve in this world and what people you were assigned to help. These are every person's life responsibilities, and the bar is set high when you aspire to carry them out. Yet we can't ascend to the high places and keep one foot in the valley. Rise up, all of you, up from the low places and set your aspirations for life higher.

During my course of study for this topic, I ran into some very interesting information that helped solidify how important commitment is. Did you know that when a pilot is ready for takeoff and taxis on the runway, once he hits a certain speed; he radios the tower with an abbreviated term? That term is "VR," which means, "I am committed to takeoff." Once he says VR and gives his commitment, it is nearly impossible to change his mind, he must see it through. To not follow through with takeoff could, in most cases, prove detrimental to both the plane and anyone aboard. Following through is mandatory.

To all my Sisters… When we decide to say yes to life, we are saying VR. We are then forgetting what is behind us and instead pushing to soar toward what lies ahead. We understand that to turn around not only affects us but will impact and have ramifications on all the lives around us if we hesitate in our course. We may get tired in the process, but we know that renewal and replenishment are always available to the faithful.

For those of you who have flown before, you know that there will be times when the plane runs into turbulence. Turbulence is basically pockets or streams of unstable air. It sounds a lot more serious than it is, but the reality is that turbulence is part of flying. The pilot of the plane does not get alarmed when he hits it, neither does he turn around. He knows that it is only temporary and that the plane is equipped to ride it out.

While turbulence is bumpy, feels uncomfortable, and is a bit unstable, it's not really dangerous. When it comes our way, it may cause some bumps and rocks us, but it can't really harm us. If you are running into turbulence in your flight pattern today, do not turn around. If you stay the course, you will gain character and empowerment along the way. Another thing a plane will run into during flights are storms. When you fly often, it is inevitable that, at some point, you will hit one.

When you are about to fly into bad weather, the captain will make an announcement that goes something like this,

"Ladies and Gentlemen, this is your captain speaking. I apologize for the disturbance; we are passing through a storm but should be out of it shortly. In the meantime, I ask everyone to please remain in your seats and keep your seat belts fastened."

He does not panic or lose control. Being a skilled and well-equipped pilot, he knows how to guide the plane through, and if it gets worse, he knows to raise the nose of the plane ever so slightly to increase altitude and fly over the storm. He understands that he has no control over the weather itself, but he does have control over how he navigates his way through it.

We must be like the pilot and not panic or attempt to land too early as we stay the course and see it through. Once we have fastened our seat belts and prepared our course, it's time to fly!

Ladies, Let's get ready for takeoff!

Be Different

I ACCEPT
AND
LOVE MYSELF
JUST THE WAY I AM.

Be You, Not Her

CHAPTER THREE
BE DIFFERENT

✓   There's Nobody Like You
✓   Oddball (Don't Fit In)
✓   Your Difference Is the Difference

THERE'S NOBODY LIKE YOU

As little girls, we are taught to aspire to be someone else. I know this seems like a hard pill to swallow, but the fact of the matter is that our entire society teaches girls to be someone else. We are taught that we are not pretty if we don't all have long hair, or if we are not. Perfect size that most of us won't ever achieve. We are taught that we should have flat stomachs and firm backsides, and we are constantly comparing ourselves to the girl next door in all these ways.

Our mothers did it. "Why aren't you more like your sister or like so and so…?" I don't think most of or parents even knew what they were doing to our self-esteem, they just did to us what was done to them. Unfortunately, even some of our teachers would say, "Mary got all the answers right on the test, you should all be able to do as well as she did." Even in church, we look to those women in leadership and try to emulate them because they seem successful. Or, if you watch TV, you will see all the advertisements showing women who we should aspire to be like. Hollywood has made billions of dollars selling women and idealistic view of the perfect woman. But the truth of the matter is that most women aren't "picture perfect" on the outside. We are not all a size 6 or 8, nor do we have the same hair, nose, face, teeth, waist, hips, thighs, and buttocks. But that's the point—it is our differences that we should celebrate, not our similarities. Subsequently, we develop a complex about who we are if we don't see in the mirror what the status quo dictates, and we feel like we have failed.

I remember one day my husband and I were going to an event. I would always go through at least a dozen different outfits trying to find the one that would make me look the best. The truth of the matter was that I was looking for an outfit that would make me look skinny. I finally found an outfit that I though looked good, and I went to ask my husband (who had become used to this practice). He would not even get dressed until I was because he knew he'd be sitting, waiting for me for at least an hour before I would be ready, and by that time his clothes would be wrinkled. So, I stepped out of the bedroom and said, "I think this is the outfit I am going to wear. This looks good on me, what do you think?" My husband looked at me and said, "The outfit you had on before looked better."

We began to debate back, and forth about which outfit looked better until he said to me, "Well, wear what you want to wear, you don't dress for yourself anyway, you dress to compete with other women."

At that moment, I was shocked. I couldn't believe that he'd said that. All night at the event his comments bothered me, and on the way home, we got into a spirited debate about his statements, and he told me, "I'm your husband. When you dress, you should dress to please yourself, but if you ask me my opinion, I am going to respond from a man's point of view. I have noticed you never dress to please yourself or even dress to please me, you always dress to please other women. Mary had on this or Susan had on that last time, so I want to wear this because..."

This would seem like a valid point when we, as women, would rather look at someone else to determine our presentation to the world. The encouragement to be different is rare. The cookie cutter version is selling like hotcakes, but if you listen to your own desires as well as to those who love you for YOU, you can cut through the noise and find your own authenticity to wear, every day, everywhere you go.

ODDBALL

I remember I went through a phase where I wanted a dog. Never mind the fact that I am allergic to them. I wasn't married at the time and didn't have any kids. I was single, living alone, and I wanted to know what it was like to have children, so I sought out a pet to teach me. Boy was I naive. So, any chance I could get, I would go to an animal shop to look for one. One day I went shopping for clothes, and while I was strolling down the street, I walked by a pet shop in a posh neighborhood. I saw the most beautiful white puppies. Fluffy, like little cotton balls, they were so beautiful. Each one looked almost identical. They were scrambling to the window, wagging their tails and just being sooooo cute when, out from the back, one of the puppies fought her way to the front. When she burst through the sea of white, this magnificent creature appeared with the same beautiful white fur but with just a hint of black on her nose and paws. She was a rare creature among all the other pups. She came right to the window, looked at me, and sat down while all the rest were still scrambling for my attention.

It was as though all the other puppies did not exist at that moment. That one stole my heart. I immediately rushed into the store to inquire about the cost of the dog—$1700.00. For that price, I hoped the dog could walk itself, clean, and know how to sing every one of Aretha's greatest hits. I hoped it could hold down a full-time job because there was no way I could afford her otherwise. Are you kidding me? I got over my desire to have a dog really quick. But here's the point: While I was looking at all the puppies, they were all beautiful, yes, but I could not connect with just one because they were all the same. Yet as soon as the dog with the black nose appeared, I could focus on just her because she was different.

We live in a society where we are all looking to fit in. Every season, some new fad dictates what the look or new trend is, and we all conform to it. Last year it was short skirts and long bangs; another season it was skinny jeans and big shirts or baggy pants and fitted shirts. Everywhere you go, you see women trying their best to conform to those trends. Fat, skinny, short, tall, black, white, Latino, Asian… Everyone wants to fit into (or out of) a label. But the problem with fitting in is that you don't show your differences. Just like the sea of white dogs, I could not connect with just one because everyone was the same. How would a potential employer feel if he interviewed twenty people and everyone walked and talked alike? But as soon as someone came into his office and dared to show their authentic self? If they'd let their personality show? A light bulb would go off in the employer's head, and he'd make a mental note of their résumé because there was something different about them.

I remember my husband told me that, before he first approached me, he would watch me every day. He said there was something different about me. He also said he just knew I would be his wife one day. He would tell me I always seemed different than the other girls in school, and that he called me the "Happy Girl" because that's how I always seemed. He noticed me months before we met. What made me stand out among all the girls was that my authentic me was never hidden. Not from God, from myself, or from the man who would notice me, love me, and then marry me. My difference made all the difference in the world! In fact, all throughout my life, I have realized that my uniqueness was my strength. Sometimes, when you are young, you don't always understand or appreciate that aspect. It wasn't until I hit my late twenties that I began to realize there was strength in originality. It would take me another ten years before I felt comfortable in my skin, but now I am so glad to be me.

Sometimes, people will make you feel as though you are *less than* if you don't do life like they do. When you are the odd ball, you don't fit in, but that's ok because when you do, no one will notice your individuality and style. Be the odd ball and don't worry about who you don't fit in with. You never know who is watching you and loving you for being just that!

YOUR DIFFERENCE IS THE DIFFERENCE

I speak about differences all the time to my mentees: a group of young women who are on the road to their own bright destinies. One of the themes that I'm always sharing with them is to embrace their individuality. It is important to know you are singularly special starting with how you act, to how you dress and look; This ties back into the stereotypes of beauty standards.

What happens in society is that people try to be a carbon copy of the next person. What actually makes you stand out is the fact that you are 5'3 in a room where everyone else is 6 feet tall! You're more likely to stand out with such a difference. Now, everybody must look at you because you're unique. Your difference elevates, and once you own who you are, you're immediately empowered. Once you embrace who you are, you can walk anywhere and change the atmosphere around you with your rarity. I don't have to be like you. The name of the book is *Be You, Not Her* because the core theme is the importance of embracing the uniqueness that sets you apart—and to show that's a good thing!

I always tell my daughter to just be herself. She went through a tough time trying to fit in. It's not easy being a teenager. She was a young 'tween at the time. She went to middle school and had a rough time the first year trying to make friends. What I told her, and always instill, is to "be yourself."

Whoever is going to love you, will love you. If you try to be someone else, you'll have to keep up that facade for the rest of the relationship, and when you show them your true self, they may or may not like that person you reveal. So just show *you* from the beginning, and they will either like you for who you are or, if not... Fantasia has a song that I love, she sings, "If you don't want me, then don't talk to me. Go ahead and free yourself." What I would say to my daughter and my mentees is to tell anybody who does not want you, like Fantasia said, "Go free yourself!" If they don't want you, you don't want them. The reason I say that is because you must be an authentic person with or without approval—that's your own freedom. Put the work in to become the person that you want to be and walk in authority without the shackles of outside sanctioning. Once you understand and have answered those questions, "Who am I? Why am I here? What is my purpose?" you will have the freedom; now you only have to claim it. You will have answered the age-old questions that define everybody's life on earth. Once you define that for yourself, your vision and path will become clear. You can be the powerful person that you want to be without any apologies or regrets.

I CHOOSE TO BE HAPPY AND LIVE A LIFE OF GRATITUDE.

Be You, Not Her

CHAPTER FOUR
BE HAPPY

✓ Be Happy? How?
✓ The Pleasure Principle
✓ Create Your Happiness

BE HAPPY? HOW?

Many years ago, a songwriter by the name of Bobby McFerrin wrote a song entitled, "Don't Worry Be Happy." This song became a huge international hit and defined an era in music. McFerrin won numerous awards, including a Grammy and an American Music Award. The song became a classic that was featured in commercials and on T-shirts, hats,

bumper stickers, etc. You could not go anywhere without hearing or seeing the slogan.

Why did this song resonate with so many people that it developed such a huge following? I suspect that many connected with the "Don't Worry" part of the song, but I conclude that even more people connected with "Be Happy." Everyone wants to be, but most people aren't. We go through life trying to find happiness through someone else's experiences, or we find that it is based on circumstances: *I've got money = I'm happy. I'm in love = I'm happy*... But absent positive circumstances, what are you?

Remove progress, success, finances, loved ones, and social acceptance, and if there's no foundation of inner joy, most will find themselves in a state of misery. Why we aren't happy is the source of global debate. The obvious is there is—economics, disease, war, and violence... basically a whole lotta evil running rampant these days. We all can't help but be emotionally affected by the news we hear, the negative stories shared on social media, and the pain of everyday life. However, is that all there is to life? If you dig deeper within, you'll find that the answer is "no."

Happiness can be circumstantial only if you put your feelings into just what you see around you. If the mood is high and everyone else is feeling good, then yes, it's easy to fall in and be happy too. But what happens when the tide changes? Are you going to go with the flow of every mood change around you or find an inner anchor to hold your happiness in place regardless? Spiritual faith is one source of ongoing inner joy; while it doesn't look like circumstantial happiness (a lottery win, a new love, a pay raise, a fun event), it lasts longer and has a deeper, more sustaining purpose.

THE PLEASURE PRINCIPLE

Happiness is a reward, but society isn't quick to hand it out. They will sell it to you— "Buy this new lipstick and you'll feel 21!" "Grab a new car and your life will be carefree!" But, all of that will buy you short-term pleasure. That is the number one drive of human nature, satisfying the pleasure principle.

From a baby who cries until they get fed, comforted, and dried to an adult who cries inwardly when the life they want seems delayed or missing— everybody wants to feel pleased. Knowing that society can be stingy with dishing out real pleasure, where can women get it, without the high retail price attached?

CREATE YOUR HAPPINESS

You only have one option when what you need is not available from the outside world: self-discovery. We talked about how little girls are preprogrammed with dolls, toys, TV show characters, supermodels, and even by their family members about what is "the best" in looks, behavior, and even occupations. That's a lot of outside pressure from a too-early age if you ask my opinion, and it leaves girls in their adult years full of other people's ideas.

In order to get to a place of personal understanding, women have to find an exit from the room of popular opinion. Once outside other folk's notions, they can assess what they want, what they like, and if it's something they don't like, they have the freedom to walk away from it.

Many women, such as Alicia Keys recently decided to stop wearing makeup. Here is a major entertainer, constantly in the public eye, who, for her own reasons wanted to walk away from it. She turned away from an image that could have been backed by million-dollar cosmetic companies all to embrace who SHE wanted to present to the world—her authentic self. She is happy in her own skin than in wearing any other.

We'll talk deeper about makeup later, but here it's important to note that the decision to seek personal happiness with the choices we are born with is what really matters. There's one place you can always find happiness: inside and living free of anyone's standards but your own.

Another thing we can do to generate happiness is to change our concept of it. Does yours look like hers too? For some, a husband, children, and homemaking is joy enough, while others would be happier with a million dollar job and the single life. You and only you know the secret to what pleases you, and you'd be fooling yourself to adopt a life just because everyone says it's guaranteed to make you happy.

You'll only know if you investigate it. Ask yourself:

✓   When is the last time I felt peace and joy inside, unrelated to an external event?

✓   Who in my life adds to that sense of joy and peace? If they are away from me, do I still feel happiness?

✓   What things can I do to add to my own sense of joy?

✓   When don't I feel happy? Is there anything that triggers the opposite feelings, such as anger, sadness, depression, or grief?

MY BODY
IS A HOLY TEMPLE,
SO I CHOOSE TO
IMPROVE MY HEALTH.

Be You, Not Her

CHAPTER FIVE
BE HEALTHY

✓   What Is Good Health to Me?
✓   Health Perspective Inventory
✓   The Blueprint of You

WHAT IS GOOD HEALTH TO ME?

Don't worry, I'm not about to list the ingredients to the best diet smoothies—you can find those everywhere. I'm about to point you to the best health secret out there, but first you've got to travel somewhere with me—within yourself. You know what your so-called good and bad habits are, and like many women, you have no doubt struggled to manage whatever you can, from diet, to weight, to exercise and overall lifestyle.

What starts within is the understanding of who you are and what works best for you. Some ladies can hit the gym at 6 am before work, put in a 9 5, hit the gym again and be home fresh and perky in time for a nice Keto diet dinner. Others would look at her like she's crazy, because the kids are still rolling out of bed, already half late for school, the gym is in the other direction from your husband's job, where he's gotta be dropped off, and what is

Keto again? That's another woman's life. So, to once again expect cookie cutter advice on what YOU should eat or do to stay fit versus other women doesn't work.

A woman used to eating and enjoying southern-style soul food may one day decide (and this is an inner choice) to change it or modify it. Pressure from outsiders on changing it often times just adds stress to the process. She has to decide what works. Does she simply eat what she's used to but now apply a "broom" of some fresh vegetables to sweep away those heavy foods and help detox, or does she just flip and go vegan?

One thing is for sure, outside pressure aside, it is SHE who ultimately chooses what path to take, and only then is it usually successful. That's why you start inside and ask, what works for me? What do I know to do or eat that will help me to feel energized, youthful, refreshed, and vigorous? What weighs me down or makes me feel guilty every time I indulge? It is being honest with yourself here, too, because that is where the traps are set, where you lie to yourself about your health and wellness. This is a simple fresh start for anyone trying to identify their own personal wellness journey.

In fact, keeping a journal or a checklist of what works and doesn't work as an individualized plan might steady your understanding of how your body and your lifestyle are uniquely your own. You don't need to follow someone else's template, so let's see if we can spot your own in this **health perspective inventory.**

✓ My favorite foods/habits/routines I will never give up are

_____

✓ My favorite exercises or ways to rejuvenate my energy level are

_____

✓ Foods that add to my energy are

_____

✓ Foods that take away from my energy
(and leave me couch-locked afterward)

_____

✓ When I am at this size, I feel it's my fighting weight and I operate better.

_____

✓ These are the preventative measures I take to prevent disease,

Inherited sickness (family traits), and problems later in life.

_____

✓ If I could improve on my health and wellness, what steps would I

need to take from here?

_____

✓ How healthy is my family and my friends around me? Do their

Habits affect my own?

_____

✓ If I did drastically alter my diet/exercise routine/lifestyle, (how)

will the people around me support it?

_____

✓ What is my idea of great health?

_____

✓ What will be for ME an easy to maintain wellness routine?

_____

THE BLUEPRINT OF YOU

By taking a health perspective inventory, you can say honestly, "Hey, your way does/doesn't work for me. I wouldn't know Keto or Paleo if I met them on the street, but I can regulate what I enjoy and supplement or take preventive measures to ensure my longevity. My way."

You don't have to do it in a gym, or on a racetrack, or in a spin class, or on a diet. You don't have to compare the results with whoever else is on their own journey. You need not feel you have to "bounce back" as fast as that superstar did after her pregnancy. In other words, even your health can be a uniquely designed journey that you and your doctor (Note: You always wanna make sure you're consulting one before embarking on any sudden dietary or lifestyle changes) and even a supportive team, if you have one, can blueprint.

That way, you can't say you did anything you weren't inwardly led to do, and you will continue to keep up the good lifestyle because YOU want to. Your body, mind, and soul are uniquely your own, and when you study what works best for you, you will always be on a path to wellness.

Be Determined

I'M ABLE TO CONQUER ALL THE CHALLENGES I AM CONFRONTED WITH.

Be You, Not Her

CHAPTER SIX
BE DETERMINED

✓ Know Your Purpose
✓ Be Steadfast
✓ Carve Your Own Way
✓ Be Faithful

KNOW YOUR PURPOSE

I am reminded of the story of a filmmaker from Brooklyn who was determined to make movies. No one doubted he was talented, but there were very few African American filmmakers. He went to every studio and was turned down by every one of them. But this man believed in himself and decided to borrow the money for his first film. He maxed out his credit cards and every friend and family member who would partake in his vision until he had about $100,000 to make his movie. It became a huge success, and now there are very few film lovers on the planet who don't know the name Spike Lee.

Determination can find you at any age. Take the 80-year-old entrepreneur who had several failed businesses, and yet failure after failure did not keep him from trying his hand at one more idea. He could make the best fried chicken, and he believed that it would be his best achievement. He stayed behind his idea with a zest that defied his age and even his track record as a failure. Eventually, his chicken would become a household name, and Colonel Sanders would be remembered for bringing it to us. These are people who knew their purpose and drove their dreams toward their destiny even in the face of opposition.

BE STEADFAST

This drive to achieve something we want is inherent in every human being, and yet some people have the notion that "impossible" is more possible than their dreams. If the course, you are taking your vision on is broken and scattered, you will not be consistent. The need to be steadfast and unwavering is as important as taking up the dream in the first place.

If you are wanting to see it through, whatever your goal is, it cannot be easily reached if you start and stop with every failure or the appearance of failure. A lot of times, if it isn't a test, it's a way to better sharpen your dream by allowing you to look at the mistakes and missteps and redirect the course better next time.

CARVE YOUR OWN WAY

For both Spike Lee and Colonel Sanders, the path they wanted to take was met with financial or other difficulties and had not necessarily been done that way before. It's almost like you see a path, but it's covered in shrubs and vines, thorns, and walls of stone in places. You know what you want on the other side, even if no one else does, and the only way to get to it is to carve it out.

It may seem as though some of these people pull their dreams out of thin air, but they are simply manifesting something that nobody else dared to bring forth. To do that, you need certain inner tools to chisel at obstacles, doubt, and fatigue when it seems you want to give up.

BE FAITHFUL

Anything worth having, they say, is worth fighting for. I say it's worth believing in with your whole faith muscle. Give it all you got. Weight-lift the doubt with the strength you build from failing but getting up, fearing but pushing through anyway. Faith is a toll you can use to fortify your determination. If your idea about accomplishment is absolute, nothing can shake it. Dreams and goals don't appear overnight. you must work at it and keep the unseen possibilities as goals whenever they are tested. How do you do this? Because you KNOW that what you want is assured. That wall blocking the view is coming down one way or another with that degree of determination.

Be Beautiful

I AM BLESSED.
I AM BEAUTIFUL.
I AM ENOUGH.

Be You, Not Her

CHAPTER SEVEN
BE BEAUTIFUL

- ✓ Inside In
- ✓ The Ugly Duckling
- ✓ No Makeup – About the Real Person
- ✓ Why Don't I Look Like Her?
- ✓ Nipped, Tucked, and Sucked
- ✓ Beauty to Die For
- ✓ Diamond
- ✓ I Love Me

INSIDE IN

Alright now ladies…. We'll spend a lot more time here than in the other chapters, and for good reason. Being beautiful is a 24/7, 365 day a year assignment issued by every commercial advertisement, neighbor, and friend. They spend more time telling women what they ought to consider as beauty and how to buy it in every size, shape, and color. It is where the self-doubt begins its slow creep in—how do I look? Do I look good enough?

It's called the copycat syndrome, every time we follow a new trend without considering whether we even like it. Beauty is both the trapdoor you can fall into from no or low self-esteem and the way to fly above feeling average.

Inner beauty has wings. Outer beauty has a timestamp according to society, and you better invest in its upkeep with each tick of the clock before it all falls away. So, here is where we dig in and round out the essence of being YOU and not HER. It's an inside IN process, so just remember that as your roadmap as we go forward.

THE UGLY DUCKLING

The story of the Ugly Duckling, as told by Hans Christian Anderson, is about a little, homely bird who suffered abuse because he was not like the other ducks. But eventually, he turned into a swan. I want to discuss the ugly duckling because it's very important that we understand that we shouldn't have to suffer abuse because we're not all the same. Our differences are what blossom into our genuine purpose.

Part of our goal should be to establish solid self-acceptance. We should also be able to accept who we are when we see ourselves in the mirror. Many women feel like they don't measure up to others because the standard of beauty is so high. Everything about you has to be just right! But whatever we have is what we're supposed to have—it's who we truly are, free of adornments and styles and presented in the original form God gave us. You are who you are.

How could it be any other way?

MAKEUP – ABOUT THE REAL PERSON When you see yourself, ask if you see beauty. Not what the magazine cover says it is, not what some false eyelashes, weaves, and good foundation might suggest it could be—*what do you SEE?* Although it took me years to understand that I didn't have to look like her, it doesn't have to be that long of a realization for you.

Not if you are turning these pages trying to find the mirror to yourself through these guiding words. I'm here to help you through the process because I have been there. Empathy is the ability to know what another person is experiencing or feeling, and I know what you're experiencing or feeling because I've been where you are, and I empathize with you.

If you are or have been tempted to feel that you must uphold society's or someone else's idea of perfection, beauty, and success—go no further than the woman within. That inner woman is probably rebelling and wants her own style—her own life, for that matter. Point to the mirror and reflect the words,

"I can just be me, and I understand that it's okay to be me. That means I look the way I look, act the way I act, have what I have, and I am still complete."

If you look in the mirror and you don't see a common/classical standard of beauty (Each culture has its own categories for what look is most desired from both sexes), you're going to always feel that you don't measure up. But if you accept yourself for who you are (i.e., exude self-confidence: Think Whoopi Goldberg again here) and you know that you always try to offer the best presentation, the world will see you as authentically beautiful. Should any other category matter? Look at models like Alex Wek and others who don't convey the traditional standard of beauty. Once Wek accepted herself, the world had to embrace what she presented. With so many non-classical styles, looks, features, and even skin tones now making waves across international media and social media, society is beginning to understand that some women inwardly rebel against confirming conforming boxes. Some women know they have no choice.

They simply will never be a supermodel or the worlds standard of a classic beauty in any traditional sense, and they don't care to be. They push out of the mold, and they do so with originality, hair that defies how YOU think it ought to appear, clothes that reflect their mood or lifestyle, and makeup that may or may not be present to finish the look—because nowadays, not all women are tripping that hard.

We understand how much work it takes to get looks out of a bottle, and more power to the ladies who invest so much time and money into it. But for the often-called "natural" beauty, no cosmetics or out-of-a-magazine enhancements need apply.

Makeup is a multibillion-dollar business, and makeup manufacturers define what constitutes the standard of beauty. That's fine, because makeup can enhance any given look (when done right—ya'll heard me? When done correct. More on this in a minute). Oh, and please note, I am not against it. I love my makeup. I love to sit in my mirror and put on my face! To enhance my own natural beauty. I love the me I can "makeup," yet I'm not unloving the woman who is barefaced without it either. Both ladies are cool with me! You must be able to be comfortable with who you are without the makeup and know, and I'll repeat—what you have is what you're supposed to have.

Spice it up all you like, but when you peel all the floss back…

You remember there is an original blueprint under all of that. It came designed for a purpose. The looks of the design are only part of the picture. The real you is a panoramic scope of so much more than any lipstick or blush will ever highlight. Once you know that fact, makeup doesn't rule you. I've seen women who don't know how to apply enhancements properly (yeah, back to that, ladies), and so they try to overdo features and wind up looking like clowns. OK, actually clowns TRY to look over-painted. These unfortunate creatures don't even realize they are caricatures of women. Makeup is not supposed to change what you look like. It's supposed to bring out what you already have so that you look like a more polished version of yourself. I think it's important that we embrace ourselves without makeup and establish truthfully whether, when we look in the mirror, when nobody's around, we see beauty. It doesn't matter who else sees it, just that we do, and that we appreciate everything God has given us—naturally first, before enhancements.

I ran into a young lady I know from the church circuit. Whenever I see her, she is always made up to the "T." I mean, her hair is always sleek., the makeup beat... then, one day, I ran into her on a Saturday out grocery shopping and I didn't know who I was speaking to... I didn't know the lady because she wasn't made up and she didn't look like herself. So, if you don't look like yourself to people, what happens in those private moments when you're with someone who you may be in a relationship with or with your family? What happens in those private moments when you can't be who you are because you have gotten so accustomed to overdoing it with makeup?

The multibillion-dollar cosmetic industry markets a certain standard of beauty because they know that it'll sell. But at the same time, it creates a problem in our society when a particular standard of beauty is marketed, and that beauty is not representative of all of us. And so, it makes many women feel inferior or left out.

Until Rihanna came up with her Fenty cosmetics line—and before her, Iman and others created specific lines for women with darker skin tones— there was a product void for some. It took 50 years of rolling dice on the right shades for many women until progressive lines finally came forward. Yet that is what I mean: If one standard or look is set as the goalpost, then every item around it will point in that direction.

We must be able to use makeup to enhance what ALREADY feels good inside us, not make us change our identity in order to be accepted according to the industry's notion of normal. I celebrate all women because we are all uniquely made. We are made to represent the many colors and facets of our Creator, and everything made available to us should fairly represent that fact as well.

I look at all women as equal. Women from all over the world, of any nationality, any culture or ethnic background, and from all walks of life need to foremost embrace who they are. Then, if they choose, they can utilize makeup to bring out their natural shine.

WHY DON'T I LOOK LIKE HER?

I grew up in an era where, as a dark-skinned girl, I wasn't popular. I wasn't considered the standard of beauty at the time. Many of my counterparts were fair-skinned, and those were the girls who got all the interest from the guys.

What that showed me was that I had to compare myself to someone else because I was not being looked at by a male. That made me consider: If I don't understand who I am, and I don't like what I see, and if society or someone I'm interested in doesn't see me as beautiful because of the color of my skin, then that brings questions to mind.

Do people like me for who I am, and isn't it important that they do? What I realized is that some of us are what I call a slow burn—women who may not get the first look, but who have such depth that sometimes a man will take a double look and say, "hmm... there's so much more to her..."

I was always that kid, then that teenager, then that young lady who didn't get the first look, but I was able to get the extra second look due to my depth. That came after I went through a period of trying to understand why I didn't look like *her*, of wondering if there was something wrong with me. Eventually, I started to learn how to accept the qualities that were uniquely mine.

What helped me get over that bump was someone who has probably helped millions of other young girls like I was at the time—one of my role models and, as Wendy Williams says, the "friend in my head" person: Oprah.

I remember, as a teenager, Oprah coming on the air and how my grandmother used to watch her show routinely. We all lived in the same four-family building, with my grandmother living across the hall. Every day when I would come home from school, I would stop over and see her (mainly because I would always smell good food, she'd been cooking).

She was usually watching this lady named Oprah Winfrey. So, I would sit there, inhaling her delicious food and watching the show with her. What Oprah did for me was make it okay to be a black woman; a full-figured black woman at that. She made it okay to be a dark-skinned African American to the world! That made her powerful, as she was smart, as she was funny and courageous. I wanted to be like her. I think that a lot of what Oprah taught me was how to be the best version of myself and flaunt it with confidence and purpose.

How do you accept yourself for who you are? How do you understand that your past and everything you've gone through only defines you and can be used to your benefit? Maybe someone has to be that example for you first. Oprah was the person who made me know that it was okay to be me because she was this powerful, smart, rich woman on television, a woman who proved that authenticity can be successful.

As a woman, she showed us that being beautiful is understanding who you are and why you are a gift to this earth; and by that definition, beauty defies makeup and outer presentation alone.

NIPPED, TUCKED, AND SUCKED

I like to know about people. I like to investigate and understand the stories that serve as the backdrop to their lives. That means I watch a lot of biography programs and read a lot of Wikipedia and so forth. One day, I was watching a program on TV about Dolly Parton, the famous Country music star, when she made this suggestion as they were talking about getting older and aging: "Honey, if I can nip and tuck it, I'm gon' get it done!"

I always remembered that, because it's really about her making decisions to enhance her beauty. I've always said that any woman who honestly wants to enhance themselves, should follow their hearts. I think that it is a woman's right to do so. But I also think it has gotten out of control, and to the point where some are endangering themselves. The worse part? They aren't doing it because it's something THEY like or want – it's like what my husband said when I asked his opinion about what outfit to wear – they are doing it for someone else. However, they are putting on a more permanent outfit when they alter their bodies surgically, so you would hope they are doing what they want and not what is the latest trend. When enhanced body parts are the new accessory or a fad like the newest hairstyle, I sense we are headed for trouble. Here's why…

I read an article about this woman who went to the Dominican Republic to get a buttock augmentation. They injected her with unsafe non-FDA approved fillers. When she returned to the United Stated, she began to developed craters and different types of sores in her buttocks, which spread, to the lower part of her body, she became very ill and eventually lost both her legs. I think the cost of living up to such standards in society has gotten extreme. This is an issue that needs more examination. Why do we feel that we must keep up with someone else's standard of beauty to the point of body dysmorphia?

There was one point in history where if you were an African American woman with large buttocks, you were "out" because slim butts were "in." So, what that tells me is that the need to appear fuller is a new trend, which means it will change with the next one. Women changing and endangering their futures for a temporary trend should take note – buyers beware!

BEAUTY TO DIE FOR

Here is why we don't start on the outside looking for beauty: We've all heard the expression, "beauty is skin deep" or "beauty is in the eye of the beholder." Well, a few years ago, I watched one of the best movies I have ever seen, in my opinion. The movie was called Seven, starring Morgan Freeman and Brad Pitt. It was a psychological thriller about a serial killer who would target his victims based on the seven deadly sins. The sins included Lust, Pride, Gluttony, and Vanity. One of the serial killer's victims was a woman who was chosen because she was vain. In the movie, the woman was badly disfigured by the serial killer. She was given a choice to keep living with the disfigurement or to die. She chose to die because she wasn't beautiful anymore and decided life was not worth living otherwise. The reason I bring this to your attention is because, like this woman, many people have the wrong idea about what beauty is, as well as its importance to their existence. This woman's treasure was in her physical appearance, not understanding that being beautiful is more than that.

Beauty is defined as having qualities that give great pleasure or satisfaction to see, hear, and think about, but many women have the wrong impression of it from birth. We think incorrectly because we are often taught that beauty starts with our skin and works its way inward, but now you know that real beauty encompasses the entire woman. The title of the book is Be You, Not Her because misunderstanding these things has made women crazy. It's straight nuts trying to be someone else instead of authentically being who we are! When does it end?

DIAMOND

Ten years ago, I had an opportunity to go to Africa for my wedding anniversary. When I got off the airplane, you could see the golden hills and the richness of the continent. In our cab ride to our hotel, the cab driver, when asked about the hills—the "big golden" as it is called—he said, "That's where all of the precious metals are. The gold and diamonds." We started to have a conversation about diamonds, which despite being considered a precious gem, start out as coal.

A simple lump of coal way down in the bottom of the cold, dark earth. Besides being burned as a fuel, coal doesn't seem like it has much value. But what happens after years and years of being pressurized is that coal turns into this shiny object that is valued more than any other mineral on earth.

I mention this because you are a diamond. Just like how one is formed, there are pressures in this world: family problems, dealing with careers, health, finances and other things that will try to dim your shine. Even under such weight, know that your light and your sparkle are going to become greater, because of the pressure will transform you into a precious gem.

I LOVE ME

You have to say to yourself, every day, "I love me." If you don't love you, you can't expect to get love from anywhere else. It's important that you understand that you have to exercise loving the inner person and the outer person too. The person on the inside deserves as much attention as the one on the outside. It's okay if you've had a rocky start in life or you may not have been considered the standard of beauty.

Understand that you are defining your own self now. You're not allowing anybody to shape such personal definitions of yourself. You're learning that it's okay to not look like anyone else, because next you'll try to BE someone else, and that's a false and troublesome path to take.

It's alright to not want to conform to societal standards. To know that everything you have gone through is preparing you for your destiny. You are going to shine with brilliance when you embrace this understanding. That's why you have to say every day, "I love me." You must also declare "I LOVE ME." whether or not anyone else ever does. That's freedom.

I AM GAINING MORE CONTROL OVER MY EMOTIONS WITH EACH PASSING DAY.

Be You, Not Her

CHAPTER EIGHT
BE IN CONTROL

✔   Control Your Destiny
✔   Control Your Day
✔   Temperance

CONTROL YOUR DESTINY

We've all heard the term "master of your own destiny." But, what does that even mean? It simply means that you have to take responsibility for your life and what you want your life to be. Of course, there are the unknown variables that can cause bumps in the road but, too many people today look at opportunity and figure it is up to someone else to make sure it happens. They wait and wait, and then when the wait is over, and it is too late to do anything, their life is almost over, and they are filled with regret. You must control the narrative of your life and the story you want to write.

The fact is nobody is going to do it for you. You must do it yourself. You must take control over your destiny. Now, some people might think that's a lot of responsibility. But here's what I think: You get to choose your life. Hundreds of millions of people all around the world would give anything to live in the situation you do—to have the opportunity to take control of their destiny. "It is up to you" and it's a great blessing! Maybe you want to start a small business and stay in your community. That's great because you can choose that. Maybe you decide to start a large business, have a net worth of $100 million dollars and live in the Hollywood Hills, that's OK, too. The point is that you get to choose.

You can do whatever you like. Different people have different dreams and they should live them accordingly. No one can stop you from achieving your dream. But dreams just don't manifest themselves they must be pursued with vigor and determination.

Yes, there will always be obstacles that arise and people who may not like what you are doing, but you can just move on and chart your own course. There is power in that. There is no greater pleasure than knowing you set your mind on something and accomplished it.

Those who live with a victim mentality never get to experience the joy of accomplishment because they are always waiting for someone else to come to the rescue. Those who take responsibility get to live the joy of seeing a job well done. Let me ask you a question: Where will you be in five years? Ten years? Twenty-five years? Do you know?

Do you have an idea? Have you ever dreamed about it or set a goal for it? Are you willing to take responsibility and recognize that it is up to you?

And that is very exciting!

CONTROL YOUR DAY

I urge you to develop an inspirational routine each morning. It may come through the power of prayer, music or meditation. It could be an inspirational video. I enjoy listening to TD Jakes, Tony Robbins, Joyce Myers and Miles Monroe. Develop your routine. I'll show you what works for me and how you can integrate this into your life.

Romans 12:2, KJV: "And be not conformed to this world: but be ye transformed by the renewing of your mind. What that means is every day we must change how we think. Every day I dedicate a minimum of 10 minutes at the beginning of my day to sit alone in solitude in a quiet place to focus my thoughts. I write down all the thoughts that come to mind. I ask for divine direction and covering over my life. I put a plan together for the day and take action. The key words are "TAKE ACTION"! In the evening I look at my notes before I go to bed at night to see all that I have accomplished. I start the next day with excitement, anticipation and a clear renewed mind for fresh, new thoughts.

I take these thoughts and envision myself doing what I desire. This is what works for me, do this and you will never be denied.

Here are 5 questions you should ask yourself every day.

1. What am I grateful for today?

2. What do I want to accomplish today?

3. What is holding me back?

4. What is my plan of action?

5. What systems did I put in place to accomplish my goals?

Here are things you should strive to accomplish every day.

1. Instill self-discipline....

2. Eliminate your distractions....

3. Set daily goal....

4. Stop Procrastinating....

5. Manage your time wisely....

TEMPERANCE

constraint, control, discipline, restraint, self-control, self-discipline
Tem•per•ance noun

Definition of temperance. 1: an avoidance of extremes in one's actions, beliefs, or habits. Synonyms: moderateness, moderation, temperateness

As women it is important that we practice temperance. Temperance is a virtue that is significant for any woman because it holds us accountable for our actions and brings order into our existence. Temperance guides our decisions and helps us grow. There is a scripture found in the bible *2 Peter 1:6* which says *to knowledge self-control, to self-control perseverance, to perseverance godliness.* This scripture informs us that we should avoid all extremes in life, which is the essence of self-control. By doing this, we develop a greater knowledge of self. This process requires patience and with patience we can grow and mature into the highest version of who we can become, which is… godliness.

It is important to be in control. It took me a while to get this, and I'm developing daily. As a child I was very quiet on the surface, but I wasn't quiet at all. People would underestimate me because, at first glance, some would think I was a pushover. But I wasn't. In fact, emotionally, some would say I was a firecracker.

I would allow someone's actions to set me off. I just didn't understand how to manage my emotions when pushed, and I had to learn how to grow and gain control.

What I learned was the ability to control different emotions that didn't allow me to become the best version of myself. I had to learn about temperance. Temperance is about discipline and restraint; it will dictate every relationship and every endeavor we undertake.

For instance, if you're playing a game with your friends, do get upset because you lost the game? If you don't have self-control, you may react a certain way and cause a problem because you weren't calm enough

to be able to say, "Okay, I lost. It was okay that I did," and not let it go any further. Another example is when you are on the job and you're working in an environment where your boss is treating you unfairly or you're having some type of conflict with a coworker. You may say the wrong thing or express certain ideas in a way that is not considered standard in the workplace environment. Now you may be right, but you didn't exercise self-control in how you presented the information. I'm saying all of this because I've been down this road.

I didn't understand that I allowed people to have control over me, that they could put puppet strings on my emotions. When someone can do or say something that takes you out of character, they are the ones in power. What happened with me was that someone would say something I did not like or be mean to me and I would react instead of responding. Until I realized, in my own life, that I needed to make changes and find the mechanism that worked for me.

That mechanism is a technique that allows me to not be affected by what people say, do, or how they approach me. It doesn't matter if you have an attitude and I walk up to you and you're giving me all your drama, I'm not going to allow you to have that much control over me.

You won't change my demeanor because you're being nasty.

Try this experiment: Do a self-analysis and be really specific about what areas comprise your "trigger points."

✔ Ask, what pushes my buttons fastest and the most?

✔ Ask, who is best at pushing me over the edge emotionally?

✔ And, why do I allow this person/these people to have control over how I feel?

What I did was, I set goals for myself in gaining self-control. I created a technique for reaction that I could put in my mind so that if someone did something negative to me, I could immediately click on this other reaction—one that wasn't anger as the first response.

I'm not saying that it always works for me. There have been times where people have been rude or out of line and I said something about it quick! Yes, even Jesus got angry in the temple, but we should not be so sensitive that we cannot control ourselves and then fly off the handle. We have to stay accountable for our actions.

We, as women, are told we're too emotional. We are emotional! More emotional than men, and there is nothing wrong with that. But we have to channel those emotion in a way that allows us to use it as a tool for good. Most women are natural nurturers, and it is latent in us because it bonds us closer to those we love. Men can be Johnny Appleseed and take their reproductive abilities and feelings from flower to flower a lot easier than a woman can. Real talk! So, having a deeper emotional capacity comes with the inner desire to hold onto our family foundations as women. In other words, having more emotions on display than a man does is not a curse or a crime. It's how you own it.

Are you that angry all the time that you become identified as attitude-carrying everywhere you go? Do people run from that. Do you turn into a blue flame of rage at every slight, or have you been told that you need serious anger management courses, and fast? If so, this means you are often handing over the controls to others. Sometimes, even in a relationship, we are too emotional, and we turn people off who are part of our lives.

This happens especially when we're looking for a relationship but are too sensitive to handle one. We need to be more analytical of our feelings before we so brazenly share them. One of the things that I've learned being married for over 20 years is that men deal with the analytics of things. They don't throw all their emotions into it either.

Just like women will use birth control to prevent pregnancy, you have to use the different strategies to prevent out of control emotions. Problems are going to come, situations are going to happen, but you must control your reactions in a way in which you can get through it with dignity and less damage. Temperance save the day.

Believe

I BELIEVE
IN MYSELF AND
IN MY ABILITY
TO SUCCEED.

Be You, Not Her

CHAPTER NINE
BELIEVE

✓ Believe
✓ It's Never Too Late
✓ Purpose Driven Life
✓ Destined for Greatness
✓ She's Having a Baby

BELIEVE

One clear fact about belief in whatever form you wear it—faith, hope, trust, or positive anticipation…—is that it comes without proof or superficial evidence; in fact, it exists because of its absence. It is trust unearned about a future outcome about which you are assured. It's like Christ's parable about the mustard seed. One viewpoint is that faith as tiny as a mustard seed (which is so small it's practically microscopic) is enough to manifest.

Here's another to walk with: a mustard seed is absolute. It and you know that, once planted, it is going to be—not an apple tree, an olive vine, or the Ford Motor Plant, but it will —a mustard plant.

BELIEVE

It is so absolute that you can plant it and walk away KNOWING you won't come back to find an oak tree. How much of what we believe is so absolute? Do you ever hear people say, "I don't trust anybody" or "I don't trust anything before I know all about it"—well, test that theory in action.

You go up to a chair in a conference room and sit right down in it. You don't pat the seat or test the legs; you sit in it without thinking about it. You trust the label on Listerine™ to hold mouthwash and not battery acid (even though that's what you think it taste like is on the first swoosh); you, like millions of consumers, might sit through the burn, trusting it's doing what it says it does. You eat food cooked by strangers when you eat out... in other words, you trust by the minute. You have faith stepping behind the wheel of a car, you trust your brakes will work. Anticipation is hope, and hope is a quieter sister to faith, which again, once established in something, is absolute in its delivery, and you never once doubt it.

BELIEVE

It's life changing when you believe in something that is greater than yourself. It's important that you believe your life has a destiny because doing so empowers you into knowing, with absolute faith, that you can have anything you would like to create for yourself.

Belief or confidence in something starts in your mind because it's a thought. But then, it must permeate into your heart in order to become part of your entire being, meaning your actions, words, and purpose will all reflect that understanding. You become the dream in action this way. Or it can go in reverse.

Something you desire or trust with all your heart can convince even your sometimes-stubborn mind to shut up and go with the flow! When you believe that you can do something, when you believe that you can accomplish anything; it becomes part of your existence. That means there is nothing that can stop you from achieving that goal. You can't even stop yourself because you've made it a subconscious part of you.

Once you affirm what it is, you will convince everybody around you that what you believe in is necessary, like Spike Lee with his movie dream and getting his family to invest. He made many people believers. Like Oprah who presented her shining best—to the world and made us all believers to this day.

The heart is very interesting because it holds all the secrets to our thoughts. It holds the part of us that makes us, US. It holds the exclusivity on feelings. It is often stronger than the mind when it comes to holding on to precious things, such as faith. To hold your belief in a constant state of love and gratitude for a positive outcome is the best use of your heart and the best negotiator for a stubborn or stressed mind.

IT'S NEVER TOO LATE

I mentioned Colonel Sanders and his dream behind KFC. We know he was determined, but let's look at how long he held on to his dream… Colonel Sanders was a serial entrepreneur as a young man.   He tried multiple businesses, each of which failed spectacularly, enough to make any other grown man hang it all up. By the time he was already in his 70s, he had a past of failures as his foundation but a future full of hope. Once he got hold of an idea, he believed in it. He knew his Kentucky Fried

Chicken recipe could be a huge success.

Although he got many closed doors, he was eventually able to strike his first deal for KFC. Had he given up, there'd be a whole lotta family gatherings with no takeout fried chicken buckets in the middle. It's an American tradition, and something in him pushed that into existence. What that taught me was that it doesn't matter when you get started, or if it didn't work when you were younger in your twenties or thirties. As long as God gives you an opportunity to wake up in the morning, it's never too late to accomplish those things you have as your destiny or purpose. If the energy, will, creativity, connections, and stamina to see it through are there, then the only question is, "What's stopping you?"

Be willing to sacrifice to get what it is you believe you can have. You will know what that is when it comes, but it's a part of the test of the faith you endure when undertaking a big dream. Not everyone will ride or die with you on it, it may take loads of investment time, money, or both, and people who are dead weights may need to be told to "go free yourself." You'll sacrifice along the way, but you'll receive the reward and payoff when it arrives.

That's why I always encourage people, wherever I go, that if you wake up in the morning, there is a mandate on your life. What that mandate is, is between you and your Creator. There is something that you were born to do that no one else can do, but you. It doesn't matter if it didn't happen yesterday, since today might be that moment.

Many times, we get distracted throughout our lives, and a lot of the things that could have happened in our thirties don't happen until our forties or later. But the good thing is that no matter when you turn that mechanism on, you understand that as long as you're alive, you'll have an opportunity to achieve it, and that it's never too late.

DESTINED FOR GREATNESS

I've mentioned that word a lot—destiny. Did you know that everyone is destined right now? When you see people, who have accomplished great feats, from Michael Phelps to Oprah Winfrey to Denzel Washington to Serena Williams... you see greatness that came out of excelling or excellence pursued. They worked at their craft or dream and pushed to exceed the limits around it, and the end result was what we call success.

You see people who are relentless in pursuing their goals. They are determined that they are going to win.

Oftentimes, it is born out of faith—spiritual or bare grit. A winner has absolute faith in something higher than themselves. I wrote a song on my last album, "I've Got to Win." entitled, "I'm a Winner." God says I'm a winner. Why? Because he said, "I'm the head and not the tail. I'm above and not beneath. He gave me the victory to accomplish anything."

When I know that I have God on my side, that's the wind behind me pushing on. I'm destined for a purpose, and with excellence, greatness can follow. It's the fuel in the lamp that makes me shine. Based on pure faith, I'm destined to be successful, just as everyone, in purpose, is lined up for something great as well. Now, greatness can be defined in many ways.

That's why I always say you should define your life by your own standards. If we look at what people say is great, we will define our lives by that. It's the respect for a level of achievement that you determine is your goal, and it may not always look like everyone else's, mind you. When I was in high school, one of the custodians at the school, an older gentleman (who was getting ready to retire) told me that he always wanted to work in a school as a custodian for the City of New York.

Some may feel like that is not a great career option, and would pick another career over it. Who wants to be a custodian? They might ask this, thinking it is a lowly, service-oriented job you would have to be forced to do because you were not qualified to do better.

Well, where he comes from, born in the south and growing up with a fifth-grade education, that position was the epitome of success to him. About those qualifications…

To become a custodian with the New York City Department of Education you must take an exam, you have to be fingerprinted, you have to go through this whole, long process of recruitment and training. You'd have to have the aptitude to pass various levels to get that position. For someone with a fifth-grade education, because he could accomplish that, he is living his own greatness.

Serena Williams could identify what her definition of greatness was. For her, it was winning tennis matches. For the janitor, passing the rigors of getting hired in a coveted job, in his understanding, was a great achievement. Greatness is found on the other end of following your destiny. Along the way, you work hard to excel, and to give time to what it is that is needed.

There is a book by Rick Warren called *The Purpose Driven Life*. It has become a worldwide phenomenon. It has been translated into over 85 languages and is one of the most popular books of all time in the world. The book really expounds on the questions that everybody wants to answer, "Why am I here? What is my purpose in life? Who am I?" Those are the questions that we all ask ourselves; some more than others. Until those questions are answered, you will never understand your destiny.

It starts with:

I am here because____. My purpose in life is____.

If you don't define that as a blueprint for your life, you can't live out your story with any order or self-design. That means industries without your total best interest get to control you. Your defined blueprint is your defense and your roadmap. If you don't know those answers before you embark on a dream, you start living your story without guidelines and getting lost is inevitable at some point.

Guaranteed.

We have a God-given blueprint to follow, but it comes with some unknown areas that we have to fill in the blanks on. The only way you can get the information you need is by asking the One that made you. The One that created you, flaws and all! The One that made you the way you look is the One that can download the information for your journey. It's important that you spend quality time and get comfortable with those three essential questions.

Who am I?   Why am I here?   What is my purpose?

SHE'S HAVING A BABY

There is a good analogy between a woman being pregnant with a baby and carrying her future and dreams in her heart. Pregnancy is a state I know well as a mom of four. I've been pregnant a lot! In every pregnancy, I realized that I had to carry the baby for it to grow. I carried my children full-term and pushed them all out when it was time. Time is the operative word here.

Pregnancy is broken into several trimesters, and a woman who is pregnant physically is not unlike a woman unfolding during each stage of her personal growth toward her destiny. Once you "get pregnant" with a vision or dream, you will nurture it inside of you and watch it grow. When that vision is ready, you will push it out into the world. That dream will grow and develop just like a baby into a young child, a child into a teen, and a teen into a young adult, meaning that a dream can also mature in its fulfillment, and time and patience through it is the key. I was heavily "pregnant" as an entrepreneur. Leaving Rockefeller Records many years ago, I was at a crossroads. I had these different visions for my life, and I didn't know what I wanted to do; and as a result, I kind of just bounced around. I was singing backgrounds, going on tour, and then I landed a label job. I was trying to figure out the terrain of life.

I remember having this feeling and saying, "I can't do this! I've got dreams, but I'm scared. I feel like I'm not able to do it. I don't have enough money. I'm not smart enough." I handled Jay- Z's publicity for many years until I didn't really want to do PR anymore. I was also tired of being on the road, singing and performing. I needed some stability, but I still wanted to be around the music industry.

I started out fresh and eager at first, but the fatigue settled in as each trimester of carrying everyone else's major responsibilities weighed me down. Initially, when I started doing PR for Jay-Z, it was after a meeting with Damon Dash at a radio station event that he said, "We started this new label, and we need some people that want to be a part of it." I thought this was a cool way to get a record deal, to be honest with you. I started working at Rockefeller Records, and I quickly found out that I had a knack for publicity and marketing. It was during the years I spent there that I discovered a hunger inside of me to have my own PR firm.

That hunger became so great that once I left Rockefeller, I got mentorship from other top publicists and did PR for many years with A list celebrities. I could finally make a living doing what I loved. But that would not have been possible had I not "gotten pregnant" with my destiny and the idea that it was my own and no one else's. That would not have been possible had I not "pushed that baby out." My current success would not exist had I not taken a chance on myself, invested in myself, or carried the pain of bringing forth something so big and so important to my purpose, and it would take all of me to nurture to maturity.

Become

**EVERY DAY, AND
IN EVERY WAY,
I AM BECOMING
A BETTER ME.**

Be You, Not Her

CHAPTER TEN
BECOME

✓ No Apologies
✓ Get Used to Me
✓ No Failure
✓ I Am What I Say I AM

NO APOLOGIES

Speaking of…

I had to learn how to stop being sorry for being me. No apologies here people! I'm an interesting character with a big personality. I'm very candid which can be misconstrued. I'm truthful and honest and a no-nonsense kind of person, but I'm also one of the sweetest people, and one of the best friends you'll ever have.

I had to learn how to stop making apologies for my characteristics in order to become fully authentic. Otherwise, people would get a fraction of who I am, only dished out in doses. I had to be true to myself.

What happens is that when somebody says that your personality may be "a lot," you should "tone it down," or "why don't you act more like_____," it affects your psyche. You start to apologize for who you naturally are.

But being who you naturally are doesn't mean you cannot become a better version of yourself. It just means building upon your natural personality traits.

For example, you could be genuinely funny. But if your teacher says, "Stop being a class clown," because you're disruptive, then being hilarious is not so good in that scenario. Yet, you don't want to become a serious person all the time, because then you aren't being authentically you.

Don't apologize for your personality, work on your shortcomings and "shine." You can accept the fact that you're the class clown and that you naturally have this funny, outgoing personality that begs to be expressed. But if you need to redirect some of your energy or your presentation, that's fine too.

You don't need to apologize to anybody for it, however. I think everyone knows when something about you is real, and if they see you stand by it, they will love and stay, or they will free themselves because they just don't get it.

Once you have accepted yourself, you:

✓ understand your destiny

✓ answer those questions

✓ have a purpose driven life

✓ walk in authority without apologizing

✓ understand that you belong wherever you're planted

There was a point in my life when I was working in the music industry very heavily. I was a well-known executive, but I didn't feel like I belonged or that I was worthy of being there.

This was because I still had not found the answer to those three questions, *"Who am I? Why am I here? What is my purpose?"* I lacked the blueprint for the direction of my life. I felt that I wasn't worthy to be where I was because I wasn't comfortable with myself. I hadn't really done the work to become a powerful woman. Even though I was doing incredible things, I didn't feel like I belonged among other top executives. I didn't feel like I was worthy on the inside. It had nothing to do with my role or position. All the things that I had to work on to find those answers and understand my direction to know that.......... wherever I'm planted, that is where I'm supposed to be.

There are people that will make you feel like you don't belong where you are planted mainly because they are intimidated.

When you don't know who you are, their intimidation can make you agree with them. But it's really their hang up, not yours. Once I understood that, I knew where my feet were planted, and I was supposed to be at that specific place and time in life, with those people, doing exactly what I was doing, that's when I knew I was powerful, and I could do all things.

When you *do* arrive at that level of the dream you started out wishing for, one of the mind's tricks is to doubt it. To test the absoluteness of the vision. Instead, relax into the accomplishment that follows excelling and the hard pursuit of your goal. Celebrate yourself and your accomplishments!

I had to learn how to celebrate being a counterpart to multimillionaires who have achieved many things and to know that I had worked just as hard as they had. I may not have acquired their money yet… but I belonged there! Whatever they could accomplish, I could too. That's why I was working so hard. Self-knowledge stems from you embracing these dynamics.

GET USED TO ME

Just as you are getting used to yourself, people will need to adjust to the changes you undergo with this new blueprint firmly in place. Some people will say you're "brand new." I have a family member who calls me during the day while I'm running my business. I always take her call, and I'll talk to her for a bit. Eventually, I will say, "Hey, let me go. I've got to get back to work," but she always responds, "Yeah, right," as if to imply that what I'm doing is not work and I could spend time talking to her. This family member has not gotten used to the person I've become. Some people are not able to understand how much goes into what you're doing, and they'll try to minimize it based on their needs. You're going to have times when people won't accept this new, improved person.

But you must be strong while you excel with your vision and your legacy, otherwise, you end up blocking your destiny.

Once you practice the encouragement coming from the pages of this book, you will be a fresh and new creature. You will be someone people will now see differently. A person that people will understand has put some effort into becoming who they are. Having successfully put work into business, health, family, and goals as well as into making a better version of yourself, you're going to become. What that becoming unfolds is fresh, but it's still the essence of the true you. But that was the goal here, correct?

NO FAILURE

You cannot accept failure. I really believe that. One of my mantras: "There's no such thing as failure." One person's failure is not failure for another person.

The door that closes for them could mean there's a window opened for you. It doesn't mean that you can't get what you're supposed to get because the history behind that dream has failures. It just means there's something better or different coming.

It's also how you interpret setbacks and necessary delays. Some things stall because they are incubating (like that baby you might carry). Sometimes, growing things need a dark phase, to gestate. You can't know its delivery date so easily, so you have to tarry with it. Then one day, it blossoms. That doesn't mean that during its cocoon period it was dead, dormant, or a failure. It was slowly coming to fruition. Sometimes, a setback or an outright crash into a wall is enough to send anybody running; but again, interpretation is everything.

There was a businessman who, on the night of his factory shutting down, took one final walk through. He examined the boxes of seemingly failed engine parts that didn't make the grade for the companies he tried prospering by selling to. Box after box of what looked like a colossal waste. Just before he turned out the lights, he looked at one of the gadgets and thought, "Hmmm, this might not be a great engine accessory, but I bet some kid would love to tinker around with it." Not long after, his line of toys, based on the same product, had made him a millionaire, saved his business, and became a household name, being passed down for generations.

You will find (if you're nosey about other people's success stories and climb through the hardships to find not just their destiny but themselves) many such stories of people flipping the script on failure and reinterpreting it as another opportunity, just overlooked. If you want success, change your concept of failure and reinvent what didn't work one way into something that can work in another way.

I AM WHAT I SAY I AM

To carry out the directive your heart issues once you have explored it to its core and answered those vital questions, you must speak it into existence. The power of life and death is in our tongue. Whatever you say about yourself, that's what you become. Fake it 'til you become it, it'll only feel false if you don't believe you actually are on the path to that success. You're simply tricking components of your doubtful mind into joining your heart. So, if you say that you're strong and you're powerful, then you will become that. I am what I say I am is really a declaration that says, "I don't have to be defined by anybody. I am what I say I am. You don't define me, I do. If I believe I am this, I can become that." Becoming begins with believing and finishes with one basic task that doesn't require any heavy lifting at all—being you.

CONCLUSION

BE YOU NOT HER was birth out of my lifelong journey of self-discovery. It's beautiful journey of self-love. A journey that has allowed me to embrace the woman I see in the mirror every day and pass that knowledge and truth on o other women so we all grow and improve to become the woman were created to be.

It is time to reveal your genuine self and expose the glorious treasures buried deep inside you to the world. Remove the shadows of self-doubt from your life and let your immaculate self-soar high beyond boundaries. You will never arrive, but you will continue to push toward your goals every day with the principles I've outlined in this book.

You are smart. You are strong. You know who you are and what you can accomplish. Becoming the woman, you are created to BE requires dedication, discipline and determination. You must be committed to the process. It's about being enough just the way you are but working hard to become a better version of yourself.

Now get up, go look in the nearest mirror, and after asking yourself those vital questions, and defining them and what is most beautiful and possible for your own destiny, look hard and tell me…

Do you see YOU or HER staring back?

BE YOU NOT HER.

ABOUT THE AUTHOR

CEO/philanthropist/singer-songwriter and author Tonya Lewis-Taylor sits at the helm of the **I WILL GRADUATE Youth Development Agency** and is also Co-founder/Executive Director of **Entertainers 4 Education Alliance, Inc** a non-profit organization that utilizes the power of music, entertainment, and high-profile individuals to promote education.

Taylor has been awarded several proclamations by New York City's Mayor's DeBlasio and Bloomberg, as well as New York State Governors Cuomo and Patterson for outstanding service—declaring I WILL GRADUATE DAY for the city and state of New York. Further recognitions include New York's Daily News naming her one of New York City's Great People, MSNBC honoring her as a Foot Soldier, and Columbia University naming her New Yorker of the Week.

As a former celebrity publicist and executive in the music industry, her work includes a tenure at Roc-A-Fella Records. A gifted and multifaceted performer, Taylor released her 2014 debut album Delayed But Not Denied, she made Billboard's Top 15 with her single "Thank you" and again hitting Billboard's Top 20 with a song from her 2016 sophomore album, I've Got to Win entitled, "I'm a Winner." In 2020 Tonya Lewis Taylor will release her third album project "I Am More Than A Conqueror." She's been featured throughout the media and has been the recipient of numerous other awards and recognitions.

More at www.tonyalewistayor.com.

Made in the USA
Middletown, DE
23 August 2020